Women Who RV
and Their Kindred Spirits

Marion Sandra Orem

Authentic Voices Productions, LLC
Phoenix, Arizona

Copyrighted Material

Women Who RV and their Kindred Spirits
Copyright © 2010 by Marion Sandra Orem
Authentic Voices Productions

Distributor: American Traveler Press Phoenix, Arizona
1-800-234-1574

All rights reserved.

No part of this publication may be reproduced, stored in a retrieval system or transmitted, in any form or by any means—electronic, mechanical, photocopying, recording or otherwise—without prior written permission, except for the inclusion of brief quotations in a review.

For information about this title or to order other books and/or electronic media, contact the publisher:

Marion Sandra Orem
www.togivevoice.com
602-740-6816

ISBN 978-1-55838-196-4

Printed in the United States of America

Cover and book design: 1106 Design

I honestly thought that Kindred Spirit Marty Hanus would be the last one standing. He was the first to fall. Rest in peace my friend…

to figure things out as they go along and deal with any problems as they arise.

The joy of the open road and their own personal freedom are what matters most to these women.

Women Who RV and Their Kindred Spirits gives voice to women who had the courage to follow their dreams and take the path less traveled. These women are special and can be mentors to other women who have thought of the RV lifestyle as an attractive option but have not yet taken that step toward living it.

They are also role models for living your dream, whatever that dream may be. It takes courage to step out of your old life and try something new. These women did it in spite of questions and fears. They found new adventures, new abilities, and—in some cases—new lives as a result.

So can you.

—Jaimie Hall Bruzenak
Author of *RV Traveling Tales: Women's Journeys on the Open Road*, *The Woman's Guide to Solo RVing* and other RV books.
—*RVLifestyleExperts.com*

Foreword

It takes courage to go off and live full-time in your RV, even more so for a woman, I believe. Thoughts that can occur:

- ❖ Can I drive an RV?
- ❖ Is it safe?
- ❖ How will I meet people and experience a sense of community?
- ❖ What do I do if I have a problem? Can I really sell everything, give up my home and live in an RV?

Having a mentor, another woman who is living on the road and who loves the RV lifestyle, can make the difference. She provides you with a role model, someone to whom you can go if you have questions. Think of her as a friend who has already figured out the ropes.

Women who choose this lifestyle are strong and courageous. They have bravely stepped into the unknown. They push forward in spite of their fears, possessing the self-confidence to know they will be able face right now," I was cautioned by someone who reached out to help me.

I am the biggest fear I face and I struggle with that fear every day. I exploit that struggle through writing and digital storytelling. My mother's love of the movies nurtured a legacy that became my lifeline.

Authentic Voices Productions was born out of that legacy and that lifeline. I want "...*to give voice*" through digital storytelling interviews. Interviews that will celebrate the voices of women who follow their dreams.

A single voice can capture attention. Attention can become the foundation for a story. The story can then grow into an interview that can be shared with others.

For me, the glass is full now, replenished by stories yet to be heard. Digital storytelling is not work for the faint of heart, but it is my remaining life's work.

My mother's favorite movie: *42nd Street*—1933 starring Dick Powell and Ruby Keeler. My favorite memory: I can still hear Mom tap dancing while she does the dinner dishes—always a magic time for me.

Preface

"Every end is a beginning ... gain is disguised as loss ... the trick is to metabolize the pain as energy ...."
—Julia Cameron, *the Artist's Way*

When my mother died in 1981, I thought that was as tough as it gets. I was wrong.

A crisis of self-confidence interrupted my daily routine in early 1993 with an isolation so swift it challenged my sanity.

Success had always come easy for me, as natural as sunrise and sunset. Dread drifted in like fog, unsuspected and unsettling, it was my mind that I came to fear the most. A lifelong ally suddenly turned enemy.

I became obsessed with the question: "Is the glass half empty or is it half full?" For me, the glass was empty.

Haunted by negative fears and thoughts, a self-fulfilling prophesy began to take hold—a prophesy I struggle with to this day. "You are the biggest fear you

Contents

Preface 7

Foreword 9

Introduction 11

Marion Orem, Part I 15

Zoe Swanagon 19

Lovern King 25

Sally Exworthy and Jan Scott 33

Ruth Silver 39

Marion Orem, Part II 45

Kindred Spirits 51

Epilogue 65

Acknowledgements 69

About the Author 71

Marion Orem closes with Part II of her interview by exploring why these stories are important to any woman, regardless of her RV experience.

Now, I've been warned on occasion, "Senior women won't visit your Web site. They won't care about a blog or even know how to listen to a podcast. They won't have a clue how to download mp3 files. Who's interested in these stories anyway?"

I'm interested, and as a member of the Arizona Book Publishing Association I've been assured, "We all have an insatiable need to read and to hear stories about ourselves ...." I'm hangin' with the authors and publishers on this one because if we don't get our own stories, no one else is going to.

This interview process has been a humbling experience. It has challenged my own thoughts about community and how each of us can benefit from these women, their strength ... and their wisdom.

Marion Orem, Part I

Sally: *So here you are with a big Web site,* **www.togivevoice.com,** *all of your own. But the big question is: Are you still the biggest fear you face?*

Marion: Yes, and I face that fear every day.

Sally: *And what gets you beyond that? Because clearly, you're functional and you're doing a heck of a bang-up job with this stuff. Where does your love of the storytelling business come in, in terms of telling other people's stories that are not fictional, for example?*

Marion: One of the things Mom said about me as a kid is that people would come up and just start talking to me—to the point where she'd have to keep an eye on me. And to me, that was just another story you hear from your mom.

Someone I know said, "No, it's something about you personally." So that was the first time I was aware that people singled me out for a reason.

There's something about me and I can't see it from in here. I don't know if it's a sense of empathy or friendliness because I'll tend to say "Hey" before someone else does. I finally realized that's my gift and people don't get heard, but they need to be heard and that led to To Give Voice in terms of realizing that's my remaining life's work.

Sally: *People need to be heard. Can you say more about that? I mean how that idea gelled in your mind to become what this is. I think this is really important— the whole "people need to be heard" thing.*

Marion: There are far more stories out there than I'll ever have time to tell. But I'm going to make a dent, and 100 years from now, I think that effort will matter to someone.

My intent was to capture stories in a way that would be put in a time capsule and buried somewhere symbolically.

The challenge is that if people don't keep up with technology we won't be able to hear these voices in the future. The book becomes important because we can still read it.

So the multimedia is important because it allows me to afford people an opportunity to speak for themselves. The only reason I'm being interviewed is because others want to know, "Why are you doing this?" Some people think I'm absolutely out of my mind, and they're probably right.

Sally: *What might be interesting for folks to know, Marion, is the fact that you have had your own RVing experience. What about that?*

Marion: In 1993, we bought a '93 Bounder motorhome. What did we know? We were first-time RVers. I know, let's go into the video business. Someone who was doing that in Denver trained us to do it. Within six months, we learned from first-hand experience that Arizona is the sixth largest state in the union. We were averaging about six to eight miles to the gallon and we were out on the road weekly. There were places we couldn't get that 34-foot Bounder into small video store parking lots.

We had to find some alternatives. We had to buy a van; we had to move into a park model; a small and very nice trailer. I now know I can live simply.

It was a struggle for us because there's a lot of risk in starting your own business. We had started a business before but not like that. So the RVing for us didn't last very long.

Sally: *You meet some people who do RVing, some really amazing women, and now you want to tell their stories. Besides the telling of their story, what is your fascination with these women who live this lifestyle—the RVing lifestyle?*

Marion: I've always been a big fan of the WPA (Work Projects Administration) from the Depression. I'm a part-time student at Phoenix College and they built most of the buildings there. I go over often and admire the plaque with President Roosevelt's name on it and say, "Here's the buildings those guys built."

I met women who did work in that era. I found that connection fascinating. I met Ruth Silver and talked to her and heard her story. I began to realize, while I may not be RVing anymore, I'm around women who are and their stories are important. Then the connection with To Give Voice and to be heard just kind of all came together.

Zoe Swanagon

Zoe: I never thought that I'd be interested in RVing again because I'd done every conceivable kind of RV and tent-travel back and forth across the United States with my kids. After that, I decided I never wanted to pack or unpack another rig as long as I lived. But while Lovern was in France on sabbatical, I had a compulsion to buy an RV. I shopped for weeks for an RV, not really wanting one—knowing that I didn't even like RVing.

So I finally found an RV I didn't want. I ordered it custom-made, and I got it as small as I could. I got a 23-foot Born Free and wrote to Lovern and told her that I had bought an RV and I had no idea why.

Marion: *Where did you think this was all going to wind up?*

Zoe: I had no idea. I was going to park it in the driveway and go on weekend trips with it. That's what I thought I was going to do.

Marion: *You get home to Seattle, where Lovern has her work in Olympia as a college professor and you have your own business. She decides to go out and stay overnight in the rig in the driveway.*

Zoe: We did take one overnight trip, and then after that she said, "I'd like to sleep out in the rig in the driveway." I said, "If you're going to do that, let's move the rig to an RV park and sleep there." I didn't want to sleep in the driveway.

We kept the house, until Lovern said, "We could go full-time RVing if you didn't have to work." So that's what we did. I sold my business and we began RVing in the mid-1980s.

I was a psychologist by profession. Somebody asked me once if I thought certain behavior modification used with kids could work with dogs. I thought that was the funniest thing I'd ever heard in my life. Then I started looking at it. There was such a market for it that I started taking care of issues on the side.

Marion: *What did your family think when you made the commitment to not just travel, but to do so full-time in a 23-foot Born Free?*

Zoe:	I didn't ask them at that time. I just told them and they didn't offer any opinions about it. They were just glad I was out of Los Angeles. They didn't care what I did.
Marion:	*What did your friends think?*
Zoe:	That was a definite negative. Our friends knew we were insane. They did not understand. None of them, not one of them, understood. They couldn't relate to it; they couldn't relate to us.
Marion:	*But what was that response about? You traveled a lot. It wasn't about the traveling then. It must have been the RV?*
Zoe:	It was because we didn't have a home. We went off and sold everything we owned, and went off into the wild blue yonder. They couldn't deal with this notion because we didn't have any roots. We didn't even try to convince them otherwise. That's what spawned the RV travel club. We needed connections who didn't think we were crazy. I felt, Lovern didn't care—she was having a good time—but I felt I needed connections while I was on the road. I needed to be able to see people and visit people and have something in common.
Marion:	*I want to come back to your friends' reactions.*

Zoe: It wasn't discussed. Everybody was very polite about it. You just knew they didn't know what was going on. Now, the very same people understand completely.

We're all good friends again. I don't know what to tell you.

Now this sounds easy. But any time you move to another community, or move out of a community, there's a lot of emotional stuff going on. Some people give up at that point. They say, "Well, there's this little thing to overcome and that little thing to overcome, and I guess it wasn't meant to be." And they give it up.

When you set a goal, you can't let little things get in the way. You can't use them as an excuse not to meet your goal. You just set a goal and you deal with all the obstacles that get in the way until you get there. But you don't say, "Oh well, I guess it wasn't meant to be," and give it up. You do it. Then if it isn't right, you can always quit. Nothing's cast in concrete.

If you look at it like, 'this is the end, it's all over, I can't change,' you're going to believe it's impossible. The truth is, you can change anything in the world you're doing.

Once you don't have to work, then this philosophy can be actualized. When you're working, things are different. Or when you're raising kids, things are different. You just do

	what you have to do. Once you're free, you haven't got an excuse.
Marion:	*I want to explore in more depth the strength of these women who RV. I'm not talking about physical strength.*
Zoe:	I think that's what binds us. It does take strength. It even takes strength to get an RV and go out on a weekend trip. It takes a different mindset. It takes an ability to get out of the nest and quit copping out on habit. Then when you go from a part-time RVer to a full-time RVer, that takes even more strength. It takes a very strong person to change the way they have been brought up, to go against the tide of their community and their friends, and to get out there and do it.

That same kind of risk-taking would apply to full-time RVing because it's a risk. It's an emotional risk. You might not be able to cope with it, with not having a place to land. |
| Marion: | *Not everyone needs to be anchored to a community. Ruth talks about that. She thought she knew a lot about community until she got on the road full-time and met all kinds of different communities.* |
| Zoe: | You have to define community. Some communities are very unforgiving, but it's still your community. You don't think you can get out of it. A lot of people don't want those kinds of challenges. So this life is not for them. |

Marion: *I'm using multimedia to capture these stories. One of my goals over the long term is to have these voices so we can hear them a hundred years from now. What is it that you'd want people to remember about this and remember about your participation in this interview?*

Zoe: I think without RVW, Lovern and I might not have gone back out on the road again because we wouldn't have had a community. We'd be right back where we started in the beginning.

Marion: *This was four years ago when you sold everything again?*

Zoe: We have RVW now. We can do this. So we did it.

   I think if I died tomorrow, that developing RVW and the Park are the things I'm proudest of. All my life I've wanted that kind of community.

   If you have the dream, for heaven's sake do it. You can always quit. Take the plunge. You have the support and the rewards are indescribable.

Lovern King

Marion: *I would like to start with the compulsion we've all heard about on Zoe's part, and frankly, we know more about that from Zoe's perspective than from yours. You were on sabbatical in France. What was it you thought when she first said, "Here's what I've done: I bought that Born Free?"*

Lovern: I was over there because I had been teaching for over seven years in the college and I was eligible for sabbatical. I had done my dissertation on Multicultural Education in U.S. higher education. I was interested in how Europe had approached this topic. They approached it differently. Their workers that came in from other countries were assumed to be going back to their country eventually.

So they taught foreign workers their own languages and all their cultural aspects. In our schools at that time, we were trying to make foreign workers become little Americans. I was curious about the Europeans' system.

I was in my little house. It was actually a 900-year-old house in this little tiny French village. Zoe and I were writing back and forth all the time, and sometimes calling.

She wrote me that she'd gone to this RV show and felt compelled to do so. She fell in love with the Born Free and ordered it. It called to her, Zoe, and she wanted it. That kind of surprised me because she always said she didn't like to pack and unpack. But obviously that's what she wanted to do now.

Marion: *You get back from France, and now you have to go to pick up the Born Free. What was that like for you?*

Lovern: I just didn't know what to expect really. I thought, 'Well, that's a long way from Iowa to Washington State.' Once we got there we went through the factory. I saw that the Born Free was a very nice unit.

It was only 23-feet long, so it was small enough that we could stop just about anywhere. I enjoyed the drive back. It was very freeing. By the time we got back, I was enjoying the RV.

Marion: *What do you mean by freeing?*
Lovern: Freeing in that you're just taking off and going wherever you want to go. You can do what you want to do, and go where you want to go.

I should qualify that we had rented a van camper one Christmas and gone up to Vancouver Island in it. We had enjoyed that experience even though we found out later the camper had bald tires. But we had a grand time in that van.

Marion: *I was always intrigued with the comment that once you two, in the Born Free, got back to Seattle, you stayed overnight in it in the driveway.*

Lovern: I got the bug from driving back from Iowa that I wanted to be in the RV. So I said, "I'm going to go sleep out there."

Marion: *But it wasn't just going to be an overnight stay in your mind.*

Lovern: No, I was ready to move on to someplace. Zoe said she was not going to pack and unpack it and have a house. That was fine with me. We would go with what we had in the RV. We had two weekends of garage sales and sold everything. That process was very freeing, too; getting rid of so many things that you've collected in your life.

Marion: *In our consumer-oriented culture, the ultimate is to have the big house and the big car and all the stuff. Yet one of the underlying tenets of this full-time RVing is to let go of all that.*

Lovern: Having a big house and collecting stuff is our downfall, isn't it? Everybody's in debt. We don't need all that stuff. We don't need all that room. When you travel all over the world, you see how little space most people in the world live in.

Marion: *Well, you're quite the world traveler. If I remember correctly, you visited over eighty countries.*
Lovern: That's right.

Marion: *I'd like to shift the focus and start zeroing in on the RVing itself. One of the things that intrigues me about this concept is: What did your family think?*
Lovern: They were used to me taking off. It didn't seem to bother them and I don't remember any reaction from my family.

Marion: *The other thing is your friends' reactions. You mentioned that you had a lot of friends in Seattle.*
Lovern: We did because we'd been very active in the women's community and had been officers in an organization there.

Marion: *They were used to both of you traveling, but RVing is a different form of traveling. This is pulling away from what people see as the norm.*
Lovern: They just thought we were crazy to sell everything and take off. I mean if you live your life by what other people think ....

Marion: *You wouldn't have done it.*
Lovern: No.

Marion: *Women RVers are unique because of what it requires in our culture to go out and do something. It's a lot simpler to get back out on the road without all that 'stuff.' You went through this process again in the last few years. What happened when the two of you decided you had to get back on the road again?*

Lovern: A friend e-mailed us that she was getting a new RV. We went online and looked at what they were like. We thought, 'Things have changed since we did that.' Then we were with a friend and talking about RVing. She said, "What did you like about it when you were doing it?"

We started talking. We really liked RVing. Why did we quit? We started talking about maybe doing it again and we said, "We're a lot older now." She said, "Well, if not now, when?"

And we said, "Yes, if not now, when?" So then we went and started looking at the different RVs. We found that since we were older, we couldn't do a lot of the physical stuff we used to do. We also discovered that RVs were so much more convenient. It's all push buttons for everything now. So we thought, 'Well, we can do this, and this is what we *want* to do.'

Marion: *And then you went on the road again. How old were you two ladies when that decision was made a few years ago?*

Lovern: This is our fourth year, so I was 70 and Zoe was 71. We thought we were unique at our age. Then we went to the National RVW Convention in Wyoming. There were at least three women over 80 years old who were traveling by themselves in big rigs and thinking of getting a new one. So we thought, 'We're not so smart after all.'

Marion: *What's the impact on you after all these years as you look back on it?*

Lovern: Well, we've certainly met a lot of wonderful women. It has really added to our lives. I feel good about having helped to start a place where women could be themselves and become what they wanted to be.

Marion: *You are about empowering women?*
Lovern: It's been important to me, yes.

Marion: *Do you know where that motivation came from within your own life?*
Lovern: The women who helped me over the years—I guess you'd call them mentors—mostly they just said, "Why don't you do this? You can do it." Oh, okay.

    Just like a woman I taught with when I was a teacher's aid. She said "Why don't you go back to school and get your teaching degree?" I said, "Well, I thought about it for a long time, but I'd be 40 years old when I'm done."

She said, "So what? You can teach for another 25 years, and that's enough time for anybody." I've been very happy that I took her advice and I did it.

Zoe and I realized that even though we had a wonderful home, we missed full-time RVing. So we sold this home and everything in it and bought another RV.

We had stopped RVing only because we had started the parks, and now we were back on the road again. We were older, but thankfully there have been major improvements since 1986 and everything on the new rig was much easier with push buttons for everything.

Sally Exworthy and Jan Scott

Sally: I was pulling out of the library, and believe it or not, this thing was longer than forty feet: motorhome/bus conversion. Anyway, it came driving up behind me and I got so excited. I said, "Oh my gosh! We gotta do this!" So here we are.

Jan: We thought about the fifth wheel and we went out and looked at trucks. Well, we've had a truck. We had a Dodge Dually that could pull anything with a Cummins engine. We thought, 'Do we really want to go that route?'

Sally: You know, I think it's a bunch of things, but primarily we're older now. We loved the fifth wheel and we loved the pick-up, but you have to do a lot more stuff. You have to hook it up, un-hook it, and level it, and those are things that motorhomes do for themselves. You push a button, it gets level. It's self-contained and is easy to drive for Jan, who's a bus driver. We like it. It's easier to park.

Marion: Let's go back to the push buttons. That was absolutely crucial to Zoe and Lovern.
Sally: Right. I remember that.

Marion: And they're ten to fifteen years older than we are. What is it about the buttons? Just three buttons that you say, "These are the three things we should know about, that makes it easier to RV."
Sally: I was going to pick the levelers. They're the only ones I know about. You've got to pick two more.
Jan: The levelers and I would say the engine retarder.

Marion: What's that?
Jan: It's hydraulics as I understand it. It somehow slows down the engine. There's a back pressure so when you go down a hill, you use your brakes and the retarder. It helps hold you back. The third thing I think is probably the mirror adjusters.

Marion: What did your family and friends think?
Sally: I don't know what they thought. They just cheered when we left. I don't think they thought anything good, bad, or indifferent about it. I remember my mother was sad when we pulled out but that's because we hadn't been home in awhile.
Jan: My parents thought I was crazy.

Marion: *One of the things that intrigues me about RVing is the nomadic lifestyle similar to being in the military.*

Jan: For me it was. I moved with my family twelve times in the first eighteen years before college. Then I joined the Marine Corps and moved more after college.

Sally: I think it's just the adventure of it—the getting away. The starting something new, the having new experiences, the breaking of old patterns.

I don't think it was the military experience for me. Granted, I moved around a lot. For me, it is not wanting to be permanent. I mean nothing's permanent in life so why should we be permanent? Why should our location be permanent? There are too many things to see, too many places to go, too many people to meet, too many new experiences to have to sit in one place and be married to our house full of stuff.

Jan: We kept the things that were important to us. Some artwork, our books, some CDs. And, of course, our computers.

Sally: I'd have to say the best part is the wonderful people I've met here in Phoenix. But you know, if I put it in the context of experience, it has to be my experience at Guadalupe, Arizona and that's sort of at the end of our time here.

I worked as a counselor with the Yaqui Nation for two years in Guadalupe. It was mind-boggling and it was probably—it's hard to say—the richest experience I've had maybe in my whole life.

It's hard to put into words. It's about being a minority in a culture you know nothing about.

I was the minority in that culture; learning how to appreciate and respect a culture that I might one day, many years ago, have felt superior to. It's humbling and it's wonderful at the same time. It's getting to know how a whole different culture of people survives in this society. It's an amazing thing. I loved it.

Jan: I joined the Heard Museum after I was a bus driver for a year and a half. I was a docent and received quite a bit of training. The Heard Museum is one of the most famous institutions for Native Americans, and it promotes the understanding and appreciation for Native American culture and artwork. I did that for five years, and that experience was very enriching for me too. I thoroughly enjoyed it.

Sally: We're still trying to weed out all the books that I decided I had to have. I've had them for so long and haven't yet read them. I want to read them. Besides that, for me, the only other thing I kept is a glass depiction of a *Zen Bodhisatva*, *Kwan Yin*. That's pretty much it. Oh, and my meditation bell.

Jan: And the cats. We just had to have the cats with us.

Sally: Pitti, the cat's nickname, is short for Pitti-sing, whom we adopted from some opera-singing friends of ours, hence where she got her name. She's fifteen or so, and a snowshoe cat. She's very shy. There's Rosie, the kitten's name—we call her Rosie for short. Her full name is Rosalia Yaquicita Guadalupita.

We found Sunny, our dog, after our first time RVing. We were visiting my parents in Newport, Washington. At that time, we were living down south of Tucson, so we just carted her out of the Northwest. She was a mix of a Chow and something else.

She loved to RV. She had a great time and she was a wonderful dog. She was a protector. She looked very ferocious and sounded ferocious, but as far as we know she never bit anyone. She was my best friend for pretty near seventeen years.

Jan: We had a checklist that we followed scrupulously when we had the fifth wheel. It's not much different from what we're doing with the motorhome.

Sally: You know, personally, I'm not worried about it. We could move pretty fast if we had to, I think.

Jan: With a motor home, you're right in there. You can get to the front. You can pull up chock, so to speak, and drive off.

Sally: My focus is on being safe as we are, with what we have, and going down the road.

Jan: Safety-wise, we wouldn't go into a dark, unlit parking lot. We try to think ahead and plan

	what we're going to do. Only then do we go ahead and do it. If we find that conditions aren't safe, we would just keep driving.
Sally:	This time was a whole different ballgame. Not too long after we stopped RVing in '94/'95, I started studying Buddhism. It was that journey that I began then, which is still ongoing, that is driving this experience right now.

It's all about, for me, reaching the point of not being attached. I feel so light I could fly. I am so glad to be rid of that stuff. It's a whole different ballgame. It's about just living in the moment where you are, with who you are, and that's pretty much what's making me so excited about RVing.

Jan:	If there are any women out there who get to your Web site and hear this and have any idea they want to travel, then I think your stories will show them that they can do anything they want.
Sally:	I also think that I'm getting the hang of the To Give Voice concept: that some people's stories are very exciting and meaningful, not just to them but to other people too, and could be told. That people like us could be excited about something else someone else is doing, and that those individuals and their stories could have an impact on many people.

Ruth Silver

Ruth: I'm Ruth Silver and I'm currently over 90 years old. I was 72 when I first started RVing. We bought a ¾-ton truck called a Silverado. I remember that well. The trailer was a 28-footer fifth wheel. It had a wonderful back bedroom. It had high windows in the bedroom, so I thought, 'Wouldn't it be wonderful if I lined the side walls with these wire bookracks?' I lined the whole thing with bookracks because we needed to travel with our books.

Shortly thereafter the transmission went out on the truck. We had it replaced, thinking, 'Well, that's too bad. It's the first terrible thing that happened.' The mechanics put in a rebuilt transmission and we traveled another 500 miles or so before the same thing happened again.

The second time, the mechanics said, "The first mechanics put in a faulty rebuilt transmission. We'll put another one in and you'll be fine."

We got to Pensacola, Florida and absolutely broke down a third time. The new mechanics said, "What are you pulling?" It was the first time that anyone asked. I said, "A house of books," and they responded, "You need a one-ton truck to pull what you're pulling."

We thought, 'Maybe we ought to get rid of some of the books.' But then we thought, 'No. I'd rather get a different truck than get rid of books. Those books are very valuable.' They were very important to us for our research.

We had a little publication about all the women's various communities that were beginning at that time. We wanted to visit them and see what they looked like and what they were all about.

We were on our way down to visit some people we knew in Florida. When we got down there, it was the first time we had seen an RV community in operation.

It was couples from all over and I suddenly realized, 'Now here's another kind of community that creates itself.' These men and women had been coming for ten to fifteen years. Every single year they'd come, the same group of people, and they were very fast friends.

They came from different places in the United States and at the end of the season they would go back to their various places. They couldn't wait until the next year to come back and be a part of that RV community again.

That's when I became much more conscious of the importance of community and how important people are in our lives.

However, the transition of going from a coupled life with a lot of community around you to then being alone was a difficult one for me. We come into this earth alone and we go out alone.

I was now by myself and became Ruth Silver. That's when I realized that I do function and that there are people aware of who I am and what my contribution to the community has been.

That was my rebirth and it freed me to become a different person somehow, and that's a very difficult thing for me to explain.

To be not a different person, but to be the same person and have all that wonderment of what has happened in the past. I'm still in the transition and I'm still in the process. There is something that lies ahead for me. I have no idea what it is, but I am free.

There was a kind of freedom that was different from graduating, different from being divorced, different from leaving a mate. It was a very different sense of identity. One that was quite different from being alone in the world and being fearful: "Oh my, I'm by myself."

That was not my sense of being alone and being free. My sense of being alone and being free was like taking a deep breath for the first time.

It's hard to pick up when that feeling was almost a spiritual experience. I realized I was not religious. I was a very spiritual human being. I knew that there was great depth to my being. I was aware that it didn't matter what ritual I preferred. You come alive regardless and you awaken some inner being that we all have but are not able to touch.

I felt very aware and very awake. I didn't feel like I was a different person. I felt like I was a rekindled person. I became more aware of who I was.

I seem to be going off on all kinds of tracks here. But somehow, when you asked what was the awakening, you got me thinking. I feel that I'm very much awake and alive at this point in my life.

It's because I'm aware and awake and rekindled and concerned. I know it's not forever. I also know there will be an end. I don't know how the end will be, but it's going to be a good time.

We cannot be alone. You have to relate to something, someone, some place, somehow. And if you have no sense of relatedness, there's no community. Community is the thing that makes you alive. Community is what enriches you. Your connection to the outside world is where you become who you are.

Marion Orem, Part II

Marion: My goal is to capture the stories of these women who RV because they're unique. There's a strength within them—a strength they may not see themselves.

Sally: *They are unique.*
You know, we're talking about women of that era, which brings us back to your mom, of course. And in one of your podcasts you talk about watching her tap dance. I love that. I love the visual that evokes. It would be wonderful right now—because so much of this is based on your mom and your relationship with her—if you could talk about how her strength got to you.

Marion: That's an interesting term to use about her. I don't think a lot of people would say that about her, but she was strong. She was a military wife.

It was my mother who put us on a train and took us out from Tennessee to New York

City to get on a ship. We went down the East Coast through the Panama Canal up to San Francisco, where we picked up the rest of the military families and sailed to Japan. We were on board ship for twenty-some odd days. She loved it. She was a very strong woman.

Sally: *Do you think you got your strength from her? In part?*

Marion: Yes. She was a role model and she loved me unconditionally. But she wasn't a foolish woman; she had rules and you followed them.

But it's the feeling and the empathy about me that people react to that I think comes from my mother. If you view that as a strength—and I guess you would—yes, then definitely.

Sally: *Talk about how all that personal history had an impact on what you're doing now.*

Marion: The community of RVing women taught me what community is, because when you grow up like I did, you have absolutely no sense of ethnic groups. I say this to people all the time and they laugh at me, but it's true. I have to be told, "That person's Jewish, that person's Polish, that person's Italian."

Sally: *As if it should matter.*

Marion: As if it should matter, but to some people it does. And it's not always in a negative context.

That ethnic richness—I don't have that in my background. So when I got into the RV world, I realized there's a community there. Ruth Silver talks about that in her interview and she has a lot more experience. I began to realize, 'You know, I'm missing something. I'm not part of something.' Out here in Phoenix that's one of the major negatives; everybody lives behind their walls and they're all from some other place.

So the sense of community became critical to me. But ironically enough, the community for me came back to the RV world. I couldn't let those stories go.

Sally: *You shed the whole Chicago scene and the corporate gig and said, "We're moving to Arizona." I see a lot of similarities between you and that move and the RV people you're interested in who do the same thing: "I'm sick of this world and I'm doing this."*

Marion: When we moved out here, we bought a business together. We didn't know what we were doing and we still don't, but we keep going. The business was in printing. It was a distributorship and it was part of a franchise.

One of my printers had a sign in his office window. It was one of those laser wood things, a 19th-century ship, in full sail, and underneath it said, "Ships are safe in the harbor, but that's not what ships are for."

If there's one point that helped me understand why I finally had to get out of corporate America, it's that I was safe in corporate Chicago, but that's not my remaining life's work.

I had it all and it came to mean absolutely nothing. I wanted to move; I wanted to live out West. I'd always wanted to live out West and now I do. I had to leave corporate America in order to survive.

Sally: *It's a nice cap on this interview: the piece about a ship in the harbor being safe but that's not what ships are made for. That analogy to your own life's work: If you just follow the story, here you are. This is where you are, and you are not safe inside or outside of corporate America.*

Marion: No. No, I am not safe. That's where the fear is. I wake up at four o'clock in the morning and I literally wonder, 'What the heck are you doing?' The only thing that keeps me going is: 'You could stop. And then what? That's not what you're meant to do.'

Many people live their lives safe along the shore. There's nothing wrong with that way of living. I just can't do that.

Other people think, 'Well, you're just wild-eyed radicals, you entrepreneurs.' No, we're not. We'll do our homework, we'll do our research, and there's a point where we'll accept the fact that you really can't see the future. The only way to get there is to go.

Otherwise, you live today and you don't leave the shore when you're capable of leaving it. You either don't leave the shore, or you live out on the ship. It would be nice to come into shore once in a while.

It's not about Marion; it's not about Authentic Voices Productions. It's about getting the stories. If we don't get our own stories, no one else is going to.

Kindred Spirits

"We cannot be alone. You have to relate to something, someone, some place, somehow. And if you have no sense of relatedness, there's no community. Community is the thing that makes you alive. Community is what enriches you. Your connection to the outside world is where you become who you are."
—Ruth Silver

The following five Kindred Spirits' voices are my connection to realizing my dream.

Their interviews honor these *Women Who RV* voices. They identified an idea I plan to explore more deeply in Volume II: to inspire others to speak for those who can no longer speak for themselves.

Marge Graver shared her experience and her support of this project. To the casual observer, she was the last person likely to drive away in an RV.

Chicago born, a south side Irish Catholic, and the oldest of eight, she enjoyed a successful banking career before walking away from it all to seek a new life. Surely there are other women who fit that profile, or one very much like it, who would ask: "How did Marge do it?"

She drew on the independence gifted to her by her mother, Betty Connor Graver.

Marge: My name is Marge Graver. I was born and raised in Chicago and worked primarily with application development mainframe computers.

I was laid off in 1985 and decided I might as well make a big change and move to Phoenix. Marion and I were partners in a printing business. We sold the business in 1993, bought a 34-foot Bounder motorhome, and started a wholesale video business. We traveled around the state of Arizona.

Marion: *As you know, I always wanted to interview Betty Connor and she got away before I had the opportunity to do that. In fact, this project idea started with her. Do you think she saw a bit of Betty Connor in you when you left?*

Marge: She has been gone now for over ten years. I was brought up to be a very independent person. That's one of the reasons I was able to easily move from Chicago to Phoenix.

Marion: *That describes Betty Graver. How about Betty Connor?*

Marge: She graduated from high school in 1935 and went on to graduate from DePaul University secretarial school. She shared a car with her two brothers in the late 1930s. I think that's probably very unusual for the Depression. She apparently made good enough money to do that.

She was also offered a secretarial position in Washington, D.C. but her father said "No." Now my father didn't tell me that when I came to Phoenix.

Marion: *Your mother struck me as very independent. I always sensed someone else there whenever I was with her and to me that was Betty Connor. How did her gift of independence get you to Phoenix?*

Marge: I think she contributed to the move. One reason I located here is that I wanted to be in a different location. I wanted to get away from Chicago and everybody who always saw me as one thing or another. This move was more of a freedom to be whatever I wanted to be.

Marion: *Do you think she saw a bit of Betty Connor in you when you left?*

Marge: We never talked about that. I'm not sure she would admit that. She could very well have because I did get up and go.

Marion: *Did any of the voices you heard on Volume I resonate with you?*

Marge: I have known each of them personally for fifteen years. Ruth Silver's comments resonated with me the most. Her thoughts came from the heart. She was very open and that's the Ruth I know.

Marion: *What is the one thing you wished you'd known before you made the commitment to RV full-time and would it have stopped you?*

Marge: I think there are actually two things. The first is not having a home base. When you RV full-time that makes a big difference. The other thing is to appreciate the commitment to leveling in a parking space, to hooking up to the gray and black water dumps and then unhooking the RV. It wouldn't have stopped me however.

Marion: *Is RVing in your future?*

Marge: I've gone back and forth on that. I'm still working full time and I don't really know. It's interesting to think about being able to travel someplace for a month or three months and just park and be there.

Marion: *I want to thank you for your time and for allowing me to close the loop on Betty Connor.*

Marty Hanus proved to be a tireless cheerleader. He was intrigued with the multimedia challenges faced during this *Women Who RV* journey.

Marty brought a real-world perspective to the realities of the book and audio choices. Hearing impaired, as are many at his age, he kept me focused on future reader and listener needs.

He treated these RV voices with the ultimate respect. He listened. He learned. Then he shared their voices with others.

When Marty's wife and my lifelong friend called to say her final goodbyes, she and I agreed I would be there for him.

It seems it was the other way around, Jeannie....

Marty: I am a senior citizen and retired accountant. Most of my working career was spent with an engineering firm. I worked in both their computer and accounting divisions and retired as the accounts payable supervisor.

Watching you master all the technology and media techniques required to properly capture these stories has been inspiring to me. I really don't know how you keep everything straight.

Marion: *You got really interested in the RVing part of this project with* Women Who RV.

Marty: I found it fascinating and inspirational that so many RVers were both women and senior citizens. The thought of people in their 70s and 80s tooling down the highway in one of these big rigs is really awesome.

Jeannie and I never owned an RV but we always felt that we were kindred spirits with those who did. We enjoyed driving on the open road with a long stretch of highway in front of us and a coffee and doughnut in our hands—especially when we were on a new stretch of highway. It was always such a great pleasure just seeing what was over the next hill or around the next bend. A driving vacation was truly our favorite form of vacation.

Marion: *You used an interesting term, kindred spirits. Have you ever given any thought to driving an RV?*

Marty: When Jeannie retired we thought that we would at least rent an RV for a trip. Unfortunately, she really got seriously ill and we never did get to carry out that plan. We were giving it serious consideration and I think we would have done it. We would have rented an RV.

Marion: *Lovern said, in response to the question, "What was it about RVing?" that the Born Free was only 23-feet long. She could park it anywhere. I hope you'll rent an RV, tool it on down the road, and wind up in a park with others who love RVing. It's a real social outlet now that you've moved back to Chicago.*

Marty: We moved to Arizona in 1991. Jeannie and I both loved to hike. The hiking in Arizona is as good as anywhere in the country. So you were the trailblazers on that. After Jeannie passed away, it wasn't quite the same in Phoenix. There were needs in the family that I thought I could address. I was needed back here in Chicago. Arizona is a wonderful place to live. I'm so happy that Jeannie and I had the time to spend there. I love Arizona, and if it weren't for family needs, I would have spent the rest of my life there.

I'm very interested in seeing how far you're going to take this. You seem to be gathering momentum here and I want to thank you for the honor of being interviewed.

Diana Hoyt has been a key resource for this project. She provided a computer-based training room in support of my *Women Who RV* journey. She and her staff offered a safe haven amidst an uncertain world.

Diana drew a telling link between the *Women Who RV* and her mother Virginia Rose Williamson. In doing so, she shared a note of joy and a hint of sadness.

Julia Cameron's *the Artist's Way* was a book Diana used to realize her dream: the founding of Heritage Designs. I too used that book to found Authentic Voices Productions.

Diana's right. Life is about choices. *the Artist's Way* offers a path for those who are willing to pursue their dreams and make the choices those dreams will require.

I'm Diana Hoyt and I'm president and founder of Heritage Designs. I design fundraising software for non-profit organizations. I'm a proponent of fundraising and the use of technology for non-profits to help them to do a better job of raising money. I'm a firm believer that non-profits weave the fibers that make our communities stronger communities.

I had an opportunity to listen to the *Women Who RV* voices. I was blown away. These women have so much wisdom, sage advice, independence and spunk. I truly hope that when I grow up I am just like them.

I was also a little saddened. I wish my mom had done what these ladies did. She would have been in her element. She was so intelligent and such a forceful person. She raised five kids. I would have loved for her to have met these women and to have been a part of their lives. It would have been great for them and for her.

Marion and I met a number of years ago. She was building Authentic Voices Productions. I was developing Heritage Designs. One of the things we discovered was that we had both read *the Artist's Way* by Julia Cameron. We don't know of many other people who've read the book.

It was recommended to me by a professional coach. I did what it said to do. I started journaling in the morning. I tried to do some of the play activities. I wasn't very successful at that. I don't play a lot.

The book really helped me and set me on a course of personal growth. The book and its influence was something Marion and I shared.

I hear people grumbling that life is so difficult, that life is so hard. No, life is about choices. You may be going through challenging times, but you decide how to meet those challenges.

I'm going through an extremely challenging time with my business growth right now. I can sit back and do nothing. Or, I can get off my duff, as one of the *Women Who RV* voices said. I can decide what to do.

One of the things we learn as we grow older is that it really is about choices. You can take action. You can do something. Or, you can just let life roll over you—and it will—but I like the challenge and I like the choice.

Michael Rosenberger is a video production professional. Media Mike, as I call him, proved to be invaluable to this project with a steady flow of technical advice and periodic "Here's how you do that!" solutions.

Mike drew on his outdoor and RVing passion and on his commitment to share that passion with his family, with his friends, and with these *Women Who RV* voices.

He used the term "kindred spirits" as did Marty Hanus. The support one needs when RVing and an unwavering commitment represents the core of Mike's passion.

My name is Michael Rosenberger and I am the Video Production Coordinator here at Phoenix College in Phoenix, Arizona.

Marion came to our office with questions about a technology project she was developing. She wanted to capture audio and video digital stories about women who RV. I immediately saw her as a kindred spirit.

I have a big passion for technology, video production specifically. I was an outdoor journalist at one time. I knew that I really wanted to be involved in what she was doing and see where she could take this concept.

My interest in video and the outdoors came at a very early age. There was a TV show called *On the Open Road* that was hosted by Bill Leverton. Bill would travel the state of Arizona and go to ghost towns, cities, and remote areas. There he would interview people about the history of those places. It really had a personal touch.

I saw a parallel between the two when I listened to what Marion had captured about the *Women Who RV*.

The idea that resonated with me was the sense of community. I have a trailer and I take my family out often. I also extend invitations to other family and friends to get them out into the RV community so they can enjoy the experience.

That was a very important part of what Marion was trying to do. I hope other people will hear the stories, read the book, and see that there is a community for people who have that same type of adventurous spirit. For people who want to be out there on the open road, this project provides a way to understand that they could be part of that community as well.

I became a member of the Arizona Book Publishing Association thanks to Laurie Fagen. No one there thinks I'm crazy. They all just want to help.

My respect for the wisdom of "Ships are safe in the harbor, but that's not what ships are for …" deepened as a result of my ABPA membership.

The association's members have taught me that I can live safely along the shore. I just need to be in the right harbor.

Laurie has known about my "… *to give voice*" commitment for over ten years. She shared the voice of one who can no longer speak for herself, her paternal grandmother, Blanche Lyle Fagen.

I'm Laurie Fagen and I've come to realize that mostly I'm an entrepreneur.

I'm a writer, a fiber artist, an art gallery owner, a singer, and a mother of a sixteen-year-old boy. I'm also a wife and have been married for more than twenty years.

The stories that resonated most with me were Marion's stories. I've known her personally and professionally for thirteen years. Over that time, I've watched her find her voice and her place in this world.

She's talked about wanting to make movies. I'm hopeful that she'll complete her goal of giving voice through storytelling by including those important visuals to go along with the stories only moving pictures can tell so well.

But you learn your storytelling skills first. She's doing that now. Once she's accomplished that, I think those pictures will certainly follow.

I would like to share a specific voice who can no longer speak for herself. My paternal grandmother lived a full and happy life until she was about 97. I hope I take after her.

She spoke volumes through her diaries. She kept them for 84 years. She was a farmer's wife who raised two children. She ran the farm for twenty years after my grandfather was killed in a farming accident.

She lived on her own until she was 95 years old. I now have most of her diaries. In fact, one of my long-term goals is to turn them into a creative non-fiction book. I want to give voice to her life story.

My grandmother's name was Blanche Lyle Fagen. She was just a dear person. She played piano. She sang.

One of her favorite quotes was by George Bernard Shaw. I had the quote framed for her and I asked to have it back after she passed away. It now hangs in my bedroom and it says:

"Life is no brief candle to me. It is a sort of splendid torch which I have got hold of for the moment. And I want to make it shine as brightly as possible before handing it on to future generations."

Just in closing, I think that life could be more fulfilling if people could just do what they love to do. Be passionate about what you love to do. Don't take "No" for an answer. Go around that. There are a lot of crazy-makers in this world who are going to tell you "No."

They are going to tell you, "No, that's impossible. You can't do that." There's that little editor sitting on your shoulder who says, "What on earth are you thinking?" You need to get past that. Stick with the positive people in your life. Try everything you can at least once.

*"What woman drives away from the
American dream
and into a nomadic life?*

*How does she build community with
other women travelers?*

*And when she can no longer travel,
what happens then?*

*And always, always, the nagging fear:
'Will anyone care about these stories?'*

Will you?"

Epilogue: "A Daughter's Legacy" Lovern Root King

Original Article Interview—1996

In *Women Who RV, Volume II,* I plan to explore more deeply an idea that surfaced in 1996 during my first interview with Lovern King for my final writing assignment with the Long Ridge Writers Group: *to inspire others to speak for those who can no longer speak for themselves.* Will that idea identify a source of strength for these women who RV?

"I feel sorry for most women of my generation who never learned to whistle or spit," resort park co-founder Lovern Root King says firmly as one who did. Professor Emeritus of the Evergreen State College Olympia, Washington, she was the one daughter in a family with three sons.

Stylish silver hair graced by distinctive earrings, she speaks in a voice made patient by life's adversities. "I was the only girl in our neighborhood and I learned my physical limitations at a young age."

Her hazel eyes having pierced six decades, she remembers a tomboy challenged by boyish play. She was left daily to her own devices by a mother with other priorities. She now sees her legacy of independence was nurtured by periods of being alone. What impact would that legacy have for Lovern and others who know her?

Every mother's influence shadows her daughter to this day.

Early photos capture a shy child at the frame's edge, a stranger in a divorced father's new family. Lovern spent her youth being shuffled between family members who were preoccupied with their own concerns.

"I learned to rely on myself and not depend on anyone else, although I always wanted a big sister."

Settled comfortably on her patio, she shares her mother Nancy Barnhart's memory. "She was a strong woman, prone to speak her mind. She discouraged friendly relations with neighbors and divorced in an era when other women did not."

Lost in thought, eyes blinking at a distant vision, moments pass before Lovern returns with a reluctant start.

Shifting slightly, she speaks in a quiet voice. "I lived a life that, by today's standards, would be considered deprived. But my strengths came from how I was raised."

Those strengths were developed in a relationship outside the cultural norm. She laughs, with a quick catch in her throat, about the annual chore of choosing a Mother's Day card.

The cultural ideal of a nurturing, caring mother—a daughter's inspiration—was not quite the sentiment required.

Truthfully, Lovern's independence was built on a foundation free of a traditional mother's expectations. Having few demands made upon her as a daughter, she reciprocated with no guilt feelings toward her mother. She also felt few qualms about leaving a Christmas note in 1951: "By the time you read this I will be married ...."

Her mother's reticence and need to keep close counsel shadows Lovern to this day. "She was a strong woman, prone to speak her mind ..." describes fairly both mother and daughter.

Lovern produces a wonderful photograph of a mother and toddler striding down a Seattle street in 1937. The mother's progress is slowed by the toddler's distraction at something just beyond the camera's range. Her mother's ramrod straight posture signals an early beacon for the daughter at her side.

"My strengths came from how I was raised ..." reinforces the photograph's cherished place on a bedroom wall. Still, whose voice is it when Lovern speaks and whose eyes scrutinize what she sees?

Asked what she admired most about her mother, Lovern replies that it was her sense of humor. Once informed of a neighbor's dog, Betty Grable, Lovern's quick inquiry echoes a question her mother might have asked: "Does she have great looking legs ...?"

No one is free of a mother's influence. What role would that influence play? Legacies beg to be explored because they are who we are. Other voices need to be heard. Other daughters need to be interviewed. Other legacies need to be shared.

Every mother's influence shadows her daughter to this day.

Nancy Barnhart's legacy is Lovern Root King. While Lovern gratefully acknowledges her mother's role, she resolutely cedes little ground in her own contributions. Who among us can't respect that struggle?

I have always been fascinated by who people are, where they come from and why they live on one side of the street instead of the other.

That fascination led me to Lovern Root King. The photograph led me to her mother, Nancy Barnhart. A passion for communicating has guided me through a writing program and has now propelled me into digital storytelling.

That passion comes from the authentic me. I want to meet other daughters and ponder other photographs and record other legacies.

Legacies provide opportunities for learning and while I am an adequate whistler, Lovern has promised to teach me how to spit.

Acknowledgements

A special thank you to the *Women Who RV* voices of Ruth Silver, Zoe Swanagon, Lovern King, Jan Scott, and Sally Exworthy for sharing your strength and your wisdom.

Thank you to the *Kindred Spirits* voices of Marge Graver, Marty Hanus, Diana Hoyt, Michael Rosenberger and Laurie Fagen for sharing your support and your encouragement.

Thank you to the Phoenix College computer commons staff in Phoenix, Arizona. Their college mission: "GO FAR, CLOSE TO HOME." I did just that.

Thank you to my Mother, Sarah Frances Orem, who never doubted that I would one day thrive in the West.

Finally, thank you to Gloria Wallace for guiding me on the path to my dreams and to Julia Cameron's, *the Artist's Way*. Gloria offered this wisdom in response to any challenges, "What is the gift in this?"

About the Author

Marion Orem lives in the Southwest and has been hearing others' voices for as long as she can remember. She'd like to hear yours.

She's learned that digital storytelling is an endless quest for technical perfection—a quest that also honors the voices of those who can no longer speak for themselves.

People communicate through digital technology today.
I mean "… to give voice" and we mean to be heard.

—Marion Orem
Phoenix, Arizona
March, 2010
www.togivevoice.com